U0100305

大展好書　好書大展
品嘗好書　冠群可期

大展好書　好書大展
品嘗好書　冠群可期

彩色圖解
太極武術
22

嫡傳楊家太極劍
51 式

Authentic yangfamily tai chi sword
51 form

中國武術八段

傅聲遠 著

大展 出版社有限公司

國家圖書館出版品預行編目資料

嫡傳楊家太極劍＝Authentic yangfamily tai chi sword　傅聲遠　著
——初版，——臺北市，大展，2008〔民 97.05〕
　　面；21 公分 ——（彩色圖解太極武術；22）
ISBN　978－957－468－610－0（平裝）
1. 劍術
528.974　　　　　　　　　　　　　　　　　97004160

嫡傳楊家太極劍──51式　ISBN 978－957－468－610－0

著　　者／傅聲遠
責任編輯／佟　　暉
發 行 人／蔡森明
出 版 者／大展出版社有限公司
社　　址／台北市北投區（石牌）致遠一路 2 段 12 巷 1 號
電　　話／（02）28236031・28236033・28233123
傳　　眞／（02）28272069
郵政劃撥／01669551
網　　址／www.dah-jaan.com.tw
E - mail／service@dah-jaan.com.tw
登 記 證／局版臺業字第 2171 號
承 印 者／弼聖彩色印刷有限公司
裝　　訂／建鑫裝訂有限公司
排 版 者／弘益電腦排版有限公司
授 權 者／北京體育大學出版社
初版 1 刷／2008 年（民 97 年）5 月

定　價／220 元

楊家太極拳祖師　楊祿禪

（1799 年～1872 年）

Master of Yang Style Taijiquan (shadow boxing)
Yang Lu Chan

楊鳳侯（祿禪公　長子）
Yang Feng Hou

楊班侯（祿禪公　次子）
Yang Ban Hou

楊健侯（祿禪公　三子）
Yang jian Hou

楊少侯（健侯公　長子）
Yang Shao Hou

楊澄甫（健侯公　三子）
Yang Cheng Fu

楊兆元（健侯公　次子）
Yang Zhao Yuan

楊兆林（鳳侯公　子）
Yang Zhao Lin

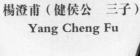

楊兆鵬（班侯公　子）
Yang Zhao Peng

傅鍾文（兆元公　外孫婿）
Fu Zhong Wen

傅宗元（鍾文公　胞弟）
Fu Zong Yuan

傅聲遠（傅鍾文之子）
中國武術八段
楊式太極拳親族傳人
世界永年太極拳聯盟主席

Fu Sheng Yuan
（The Son of Fu Zhong Wen）
Chinese Wushu level 8
Cognation descendant of
Yang Style Taijiquan

傅清泉（傅聲遠之子）
中國武術七段
楊式太極拳親族傳人
世界永年太極拳聯盟副主席

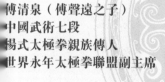

Fu Qing Quan
（The Son of Fu Sheng Yuan）
Chinese Wushu level 7
Cognation descendant of Yang
Style Taijiquan

楊澄甫老師與弟子傅鍾文
Master Yang Chengfu and disciple
Fu Zhongwen

楊澄甫老師與弟子傅鍾文在廣州
Master Yang Chengfu and disciple
Fu Zhongwen in Guangzhou

1932年傅鍾文跟隨老師楊澄甫到廣州市政府教拳
Fu Zhongwen and his master Yang Chengfu taught Taijiquan at
Government of Guangzhou City in 1932

傅鍾文　Fu Zhong Wen

傅聲遠和師伯崔毅士（中）、
牛春明（右）老師在上海
Fu Shengyuan and his senior
master Cui Yishi, master Niu
Chunming at Shanghai

傅鍾文與傅聲遠推手
Tuishou between Fu Zhongwen and Fu Shengyuan

傅聲遠傅鍾文父子在香港
Father Fu Zhongwen and son
Fu Shengyuan at Hong Kong

傅氏三代在楊祿禪故居練拳
Three Fu generations practice Taijiquan
at former residence of Yang Luchan

澳大利亞總理霍克親切會見傅氏父子
Australian Prime Minister Mr. Bob
Hawk gave an interview to father
and son of Fu

中華全國體育總會顧問徐才與傅聲遠合影
Group photo of Xu Cai, adviser of
Chinese Sport Association, and Fu
Shengyuan

高歌武術文化

徐才

12年前，聲遠先生所著《嫡傳永年楊式太極拳》面市時，我曾於他寫過一篇短序《將武術獻給世界》以示祝賀。兩年前國際武術聯合會隨著武術在世界蓬勃發展之勢，決定每年5月爲「世界太極拳月」。今年在這個「世界太極拳月」裡，聲遠先生傳出喜訊，他又有幾本新書即將付梓，並再邀我爲之作序。我深爲這位移民海外的中華赤子之心所感動，所以接受了這項囑托。

我首先要向已是76歲高齡的聲遠先生致敬：您眞老當益壯，老有所爲。從您的作爲又能看到您教子有方，代代相傳祖業的心路。眞是上天不負苦心人。傅鍾文、傅聲遠、傅清泉太極世家三代人，定當一代勝似一代。

20年前，聲遠先生懷著把太極拳弘揚海外的虔誠之心移民澳洲。時間催人老，也催人的事業興。聲遠到了澳洲不顧年齡增長奮力進取，把太極拳這個中華武術的品牌在四十多個國家傳播得風風火火，他以澳洲爲立足點，每年教遊四方。這正如美國著名的未來學家奈斯比特（John Naisbitt）在《亞洲大趨勢》書中所說：「西方正在學習適應東方化，而澳洲則首當其衝。」聲遠先生在海外傳拳授拳，就像他的父親傅鍾文大師那樣，不只是傳技而且傳理，還要傳德。這「三傳」是聲遠先生執教之道，也是他爲人師品。我衷心祝願海內外熱心傳播中華武術的朋友，在「三傳」上狠下功夫，努力把中華武技、武理、武德廣泛撒播人世間。

聲遠先生在海外授拳創業，20年可謂成績斐然。這些年他勇於探索，勤於筆耕，以圖書和影帶形式向海內外習武者貢獻了太極拳的文化財富。在多元化的當今世界，不同文化的交流與交融是個大趨勢。不久前我從報紙上讀到一篇文章說：「與中國對外貿易『出超』相比，中國的對外文化交流和傳播則是嚴重『入超』，存在『文化赤字』。」這個論斷引起我強烈共鳴。是啊！中國是具有五千年歷史的文明古國，有著十分豐富的文化遺產，如今中國人民又在創造著嶄新的文化財富。爲什麼在文化「出口」方面我們處在一種弱勢狀態呢？這恐怕與我們對固有的文化強勢認識不足，對人類文化的互相凝聚，彼此滲透認識不足有關。

這裡說一個至今仍然能鼓舞國人奮力傳播中華文化的一位先輩人士，他就是清末在西方世界彌漫著歧視中國、歧視中華文化的氛圍下，率先以流暢的法文撰寫《中國人自畫像》、《中國人的快樂》、《中國戲劇》等書，向世界介紹中國和中華文化的陳季同。陳季同是福建人，他與同屬閩籍的辜鴻銘、林語堂是近代中國人用西文向世界介紹中國和中華文化的「福建三傑」。他們的作爲對當今盛世中國的文人武士具有莫大的啓示意義。可喜的是在中華武術走向世界的潮流中，已經出現一批以精湛的拳術和深情的筆墨向世界展示武術風采的專家，聲遠先生就是其中之一。我深切期望海內外武術家攜手高歌武術文化，造福於人類的健康、益智、修性，共創和諧社會和和諧世界！

2006 年 5 月於北京

太極劍練習之要點
Important Points in Your Practice
of the Tai Chi Sword

1. 頭部要「虛靈頂勁」
Hold the head straight with ease

所謂虛靈頂勁，就是說，頭要自然，正直，不可用強勁，而精神要提得起，目光要向前平視，要看得遠，口要似開非開，似閉非閉，口呼鼻吸，任其自然。

When you practice the Tai Chi sword, hold your head erect to enable the spirit to rise. The head and neck are held naturally straight without using hard force. Gaze out at eye level as if looking into the horizon, being concentrated but lively. The mouth is neither open nor closed with tight lips. Breathe in through the nose and out through the mouth naturally without forcing your braeth.

2. 身軀要中正而不倚，脊梁與尾閭要垂直而不偏
Hold the body straight from the crown of the head to the coccyx

在動作變化中，必須做到含胸拔背，沉肩轉腰之要領，初學時一定要注意，否則日子久了，成了習慣就很難改了。

The body needs to be straight. Pay attention to the spine, expecially the cooccyx. When you first learn, it is important to keep the chest relaxed and the back raised, shoulders dropped, and the waist turning. If not, bad habits formed in these areas will be hard to correct. If your practice is inaccurate, you will not obtain the desired results, even though you spend a lot of time and energy.

3. 兩臂關節都要放鬆，要沉肩墜肘
Sink the shoulders and the elbows

所謂「沉肩」，肩要鬆開而下垂，如果不鬆垂，兩臂扛起，氣也必定隨之向上，全身也就不得力了；所謂墜肘，一定要往下鬆墜，肘如果向上抬起，肩也就不能下沉。「掌」必須自然伸張。「手尖」要微微伸屈，凡做「雙指」併攏動作時，手指必須自然伸直。

The shoulders should relax and hang downwards. If the shoulders are raised, the chi will rise and the body will not be able to issue power. The elbows must also relax and point downwards. If the elbows are raised, the shoulders will become tense. The fingers should be held naturally straight, not rigid.

4. 手腕　Wrists

手腕的運用最多，所以必須特別注意手腕的運用方式，手握劍柄不能太緊，要鬆而活。更要掌握劍的運轉變化，就能做到隨心所欲，運用自如。反之，將會導致呆板，手腕不靈活。在完成動作的點、撩、刺等勁力時，應

將內勁貫於手腕，在此一剎那間必須以手緊握劍柄，動作再變換時，手又放鬆，如此周而復始地完成整套動作。

The correct use of the wrists is of great importance in Tai Chi sword. The sword should be not to be held too slightly, otherwise it will not look relaxed and alive. It is important that your grip enables the sword to move freely. Once you are holding the sword correctly, then you will be able to move it naturally according to your intention. If not, your wrist will lock and the movement of the sword will be stiff. At the end of the movements which require power such as pointing, chopping, slicing, and stabbing, you need to put the jin in the wrist and tighten the grip at the end. When you go on to another movement, your grip needs to be relaxed. Depending on the situation, you loosen or tighten the grip as necessary throughout the form. (*Jin–as a result of correct and daily practice of the authentic Yang Style Tai Chi form, you will gradually develop this power called jin, which is different from hard force. You will only experience jin when your practice has reached a certain level of maturity.)

5. 鬆腰　Relax the waist

腰為一身之主宰，能「鬆腰」，足就有力量，下盤就穩固。每個動作的虛實變化全由腰轉動，在練習中動作有不得力處，這與鬆腰不開有很大關係。

The waist is the commander of the body. If the waist is relaxed and loosened, your legs will be stable enabling you to issue power. Changes in solid and empty derive from the movement of the waist. If you lack power in your movements, check that your waist is relaxed and not leaning in any way.

6. 分清虛實　Distinguishing solid from empty

兩腿必須虛實分清，太極拳術以分虛實為第一義，太極劍也是如此。如全身重量坐於右腿時，則右腿為實，左腿為虛；全身重量坐於左腿時，則左腿為實，右腿為虛。能分清虛實，動作轉換就輕靈自如，避免板滯；如虛實不清，邁步就重滯不活。所謂虛者，並非虛無，其勢還沒有斷，仍留有伸縮變化之餘意；所謂實者，不能過分用猛力之意，只是充實而已，身軀前撲，就失去中正。

Distinguishing solid from empty is a fundamental principle of the Tai Chi form, which applies equally to the sword. If your body sits in your right leg, then your right leg is solid and your left leg is empty, and vice versa.

7. 似貓行　Moving like a cat

兩腳的前進後退，忽左忽右變換時，必須起落猶似貓行，起步落步，腳尖點地要輕靈。

Whenever you move forward or backward, or change direction to the right or left, your stepping needs to be light and stable like that of a cat. Always ensure that the toes of the empty leg touch the ground very lightly.

8. 要「貫串一氣」 Continuity

太極劍與練太極拳一樣用意不用力，身體各部都要協調一致，上下相隨，一動無有不動，要注意劍法和手法、步法、眼神的密切配合，整個套路自始至終相連不斷，一氣呵成。

As in the Tai Chi form, when you practice the sword you need to keep the movements continuous. Use your intention to lead the movement, not hard force. Coordinate every part of your body. Seek serenity in the movement. You need to pay attention to the arm which is holding the sword, the other arm, your stepping, and your gaze, so that they are in harmony. Form the beginning to the end, the whole form needs to be as smooth as one breath.

9. 速度 Speed

如何掌握速度的快慢問題。在初學時，宜慢不宜快。與初學太極拳一樣，需認真把握好每一個動作的準確性，在整個套路完成以後，再經過一段時間的熟練過程，然後就可以加快速度。但不能只圖快而忽略了每一個動作的完整性，同時還要保持速度的快慢均勻，不要有忽快忽慢、快慢不均和遲鈍的現象。一般練一套時間在 2 分鐘至 3 分鐘左右。

When you first learn, it is better to go slow than fast. Just like learning the Tai Chi form, pay attention to the accuracy of the movement. After some time when you become familiar with your sword form, then you can practice it a bit faster. However, you must finish every movement accurately and properly. The speed needs to be smooth throughout; not suddenly too fast with some movements and too slow with others.If the correct speed is not understood, then the form will apper rushed or sluggish. It takes approximately three minutes to do the form.

10. 鬆開自然　Be natural

全身關節必須鬆開自然，口腹不可閉氣，四肢腰腿不可起強勁，精神能提得起，自然舉動輕靈，心要靜，思想集中，將意識貫注到動作上去。

Make sure that you are moving all the joints in each movement. Keep relaxed and natural.Don't try to hold or force the breath. Your mouth and abdomen should stay naturally relaxed. Avoid using hard force with the four limbs and waist. All movements should look lively and spirited. The mind should be quiet and focussed, constantly directing even the smallest movement.

11. 練習時間及地點　General training tips

每日起床後或睡前先練二至三遍太極劍或太極刀，再進行太極拳的練習。如有條件，一日之中多練幾次更好。但必須注意醉後、飽食後不宜鍛鍊。練習地點以庭園或廳堂，空氣流通，光線充足為好，必須避忌對吹之烈風，與有陰濕霉氣之場所。因為身體在運動中，呼吸必然深長，汗毛孔開放，故烈風與霉氣如吸入腹中，將有害肺臟，容

易得病。在練習過程中如出汗過多，切忌脫衣、裸體，或用冷水沖洗。無論冬夏練習時服裝以長袖，長褲為宜。

Besides your Tai Chi form, it is recommended that one practices the Tai Chi or sabre two to three times in the morning, or night. If you have the time, do more repetitions. Don't practice on a full stomach or after consuming too much alcohol. It is more beneficial to practice outdoors or where there is plenty of fresh air. Avoid practice in a windy area or a damp place. During your Tai Chi session, your breathing will naturally deepen and the negative effects of dampness, wind or foul air. Even though you may be perspiring, it is inadvisable to take your top off or to have a cold shower immediately. It is advisable to wear a long sleeved top to practice in both winter and summer.

太極劍動作名稱

預備勢
1. 三環套月（接劍式）
2. 魁星式（獨立反刺）
3. 燕子抄子（撲步橫掃）
4. 左右邊攔掃（向左右平帶）
5. 小魁星式（左虛步撩）
6. 燕子入巢（弓步直刺）
7. 靈貓捕鼠（墊步前躍下刺）
8. 鳳凰抬頭（弓步平跳）
9. 黃蜂入洞（轉身下刺）
10. 鳳凰右展翅（弓步右掃）
11. 小魁星（左虛步撩）
12. 鳳凰左展翅（左弓步右點）
13. 等魚勢（虛步點劍）
14. 左右龍行式（左右前刺）
15. 宿鳥投林（獨立上刺）
16. 烏龍擺尾（虛步下戳）
17. 青龍出水（左弓步刺）
18. 風捲荷葉（轉身斜帶）
19. 左右獅子抬頭（退步左右橫掃）
20. 虎抱頭（提膝捧劍）
21. 野馬跳澗（墊步前遠跳下刺）
22. 勒馬式（右側背劍式）

23. 指南針（弓步直刺）

24. 左右迎風撣塵（左右弓步攔點）

25. 順水推舟（進步反刺）

26. 流星趕月（反身回點）

27. 天馬飛瀑（虛步點劍）

28. 挑簾式（獨立平托）

29. 左右車輪（左右輪掃，弓步前點）

30. 燕子銜泥（虛步點劍）

31. 大鵬展翅（撤步右橫掃）

32. 海底撈月（右弓步撩）

33. 懷中抱月（退步拖劍）

34. 哪吒探海（獨立下刺）

35. 犀牛望月（弓步平托劍）

36. 射雁式（虛步回抽）

37. 青龍現爪（跟步平刺）

38. 鳳凰雙展翅（左右橫掃）

39. 左右跨攔（左右平托劍）

40. 射雁式（虛步回抽）

41. 白猿獻果（虛步橫點劍）

42. 左右落花（左右退掃）

43. 玉女穿梭（劍身弓步下刺）

44. 白虎攪尾（轉身上挑）

45. 魚跳龍門（墊步上跳前下刺）

46. 左右烏龍絞柱（左絞掃，右絞點）

47. 仙人指路（弓步劍下刺）

48. 朝天一柱香（弓步豎劍）

49. 風掃梅花（旋轉平掃）

50. 牙笏式（上步前上刺）

51. 抱劍歸原

The Sequence Of Sword Movements

Opening Stance

1. Three Rings Envelope The Moon

2. The Big Dipper

3. Swallow Dives On Water

4. Parry To The Right And Left

5. The Little Dipper

6. Swallow Returns To The Nest

7. Spirited cat Catches the Mouse

8. Phoenix Raises Its Head

9. Yellow Bee Enters The Hive

10. Phoenix Spreads Right Wing

11. The Little Dipper

12. Phoenix Spreads Left Wing

13. Waiting For The Fish

14. Dragon Goes Left And Right

15. Bird Returns To The Wood

16. Dragon Swings Its Tail

17. Dragon Emerges From Water

18. Lotus Leaf Blown By The Wind

19. Lion Shakes Its Head Left & Right

20. Tiger Holds Its Head

21. Wild Horse Jumps Over River

22. Rein In The Horse

預備勢（1-3 圖）

預備勢

　　設面南背北方向，兩腳尖向南，雙腳與肩等寬平行站立。左手反持劍垂於身體左側，食指中指緊貼劍把，其餘三指自然而握。右手手心向裏自然下垂。眼睛平視前方。（圖1-3）

　　【注意】：

　　直立時要含胸拔背，尾閭中正，自然而立，呼吸自然，手握劍不要太緊。劍要豎直，不可左右歪斜或貼靠身體。

3

Openg Stance

Stand with toes in line in a shoulder-width stance facing south. Hold the sword upright in your left hand, your first and middle fingers along the handle and your thumb and other fingers around the handle. Your left palm faces south. Your right palm faces towards your right leg naturally. Look horizontally ahead into the distance. (Fig1-3)

Point to note :
- Do not puff out your chest.
- Align your spine vertically.
- Stand naturally
- Do not grip the sword tightly.
- Hold the sword vertically, not too close to the body.
- Breathe naturally.
- The mention of the "irst and middle" fingers or "wo fingers" pointing through out this book always refers to the index and second fingers.

4

5

一、三環套月（4–8 圖）

一、三環套月（接劍式）

1. 兩臂呈弧狀自然抬起，到與肩等高時，反身旋轉45度。

2. 重心移於右腿，同時微屈。左腿自然抬起，腳尖下垂。同時左手握劍平舉胸前，右手中食劍指併攏向西南方，眼睛與劍指所指方向一致。

3. 左腿向東伸成弓步，身體向東轉90度，同時左手握劍隨身體繞至臂後，右手劍指曲至耳前並向前平推，然後成坐腕，劍指上翹，眼睛正視前方。（圖4）

4. 左腳以腳跟為軸向東北轉腳尖。左腿微屈，右腳提至體前，腳尖點地成虛步。上身中正，左手提劍向前，右手向胸前畫弧，扶持劍穗。（圖5）

6

5. 右腳抬起，腳跟著地，腳尖向東南方轉 45 度，左腳向前上步成弓步。分手畫弧，成交劍式，此時劍鋒平指北方。（圖 6-8）

【注意】：

尾閭中正，呼吸自然，含胸拔背，虛實分清，思維集中，動作連貫，眼睛平視前方。

7

1 Three Rings Envelope The Moon

Raise both arms forward naturally to shoulder height, palms up (Fig 4).

Circle both hands at 45 degrees and drop them to your sides, bringing the sword behind your left arms. Hold the sword vertically upwards using the same grip as before, left palm facing north (Fig 5).

Sit on your right leg. Raise your left leg, left toes pointing down. Raise your left hand in front of your chest. At this stage, your left hand points west while the sword points east. Your right hand (two fingers) points southwest (Fig 6).

Step eastwards with your left leg, turning your body 90 degrees to the left to take up a bow stance facing east. Your left arm follows your body to the left holding the sword vertically by your side. Your right hand (two fingers) points east (Fig 7).

8

Pivot on your left heel to the northeast. Left leg is solid. Put your right toes forward lightly on the ground. Right leg is empty. Keep your body straight. Take the sword forward as you bring your right hand towards your chest in a circular motion to hold the tassel（Fig 6）.

Withdraw your right foot and release the tassel（Fig 7）.

Step forward onto your right leg, toes pointing southeast（Fig 8）.

Step forward with the left leg into a bow stance facing east. Circle your arms orward to cover your left hand with your right hand. At this stage, the sword points north（Fig 9）.

27

Points to note ：
- Keep your back straight.
- Hreathe naturally.
- Lelax your chest.
- Keep empty and solid clearly defined.
- Look horizontally into the distance.

9

10

二、魁星式（9–13圖）

二、魁星式（獨立反刺）

1. 左腿以腳跟為軸，向南轉 90 度，右腳抬起，落地與左腳成 45 度，同時劍交右手，右手握劍，由身前畫弧轉腕挑劍，左手劍指（中指、食指）配合右手直指右腕。

2. 右手從上繞圈，舉劍指向正東方，左手配合，自右而左繞圈坐腕，同時左腿提膝，腳尖下垂，右腳腳尖指向東南，右腿自然直立。（圖 9–13）

【注意】：

眼要遠視前方，獨立時立勢要穩，但不可緊張用力，放鬆而有精神，舉劍要平直。

11   12

2 The Big Dipper

Pivot 90 degrees on your left heel to point the left toes south.
Take the sword with your right hand (Fig 9) .

Raise your right leg and bring it towards your left leg. (Fig 10) .

Place your right leg on the ground, toes pointing southeast. Raise
your left heel (Fig 11) .

Point the sword to the west at waist level (Fig 12) .

Raise your left leg. Point the sword to the east at head level. Your
left hand (two fingers) follows the sword, two fingers pointing up as
left hand sits on its wrist. Left knee points up as left toes point down.
Right toes point southeast. Stand naturally straight on your right leg
(Fig 13) .

29

13

Points to note：
- Look horizontally forward into the distance.
- Relax with spirit.
- Maintain a steady balance on one leg.
- Right elbow relaxes and points down.

三、燕子抄水（14–16 圖）

三、燕子抄水（撲步橫掃）

1. 右臂屈肘，落大臂，向西南斜上方點劍，左手屈肘配合，食指和中指併攏，直指右腕，目光和劍尖所指方向一致。（圖 14）

2. 身體重心下降，落劍畫弧向東北方向橫點，左腳向東北方向伸出成弓步，左手畫弧上撩，劍指上翹。（圖 15–16）

【注意】：

點劍時要向上，畫弧要明顯，弓步忌「丁」字，左手配合要協調（上撩時注意垂肘）。

16

3 Swallow Dives On Water

Circle the sword towards the southwest to cut downwards. Left hand (two fingers) points towards sword. Left elbow bends naturally. First and middle fingers of left hand touch each other. They are near the right wrist but not touching it. Look in the direction of the sword which points diagonally up (Fig 14).

Sink your body. At the same time, lower the sword. (Fig 15).

Raise the sword, turning towards the northeast to cut horizontally. Step forward into a bow stance with your left leg, left toes pointing northeast. Left hand (two fingers) circle down and up (Fig 16).

Points to note :

- Sword points diagonally upwards.
- Precisely control the sword movements.
- Do not make your stance too narrow.
- Coordination left and right hand movements.

17

四、左右邊攔掃（17–18圖）

四、左右邊攔掃（向左右平帶）

1. 抬右腿向東南上步，成弓步，同時翻劍向東南平推，左手劍指配合點右腕，眼睛向前方平視。（圖17）

2. 抬左腿向東北上步，成弓步，同時翻劍向東北平推，左手配合，劍指點右腕。（圖18）

18

4 Parry To The Right And Left

Step to the southeast with your right leg into a bow stance. Turn your right palm down and parry to the southeast with the sword held horizontally. Left hand (two fingers) follows the right wrist. Look horizontally forward, rather than upwards or downwards (Fig 17).

Step to the northeast with your left leg into a bow stance. Turn your right palm up and parry to the northeast with the sword held horizontally. Left hand (two fingers) follows the right wrist (Fig 18).

Points to note :

- Do not pause between steps 1&2.
- Coordinate hand and leg movements.

五、小魁星式（左虛步撩）

抬右腿向東南上步，同時繞腕向東南提劍，劍尖朝斜下，同時左腳向東南上步成虛步，重心坐於右腿，左手配合，劍指點右腕。（圖19）

【注意】：

尾閭中正，虛實分清，含胸拔背。眼視前方，提劍時劍尖要朝斜下。

5 The Little Dipper

Sit on your left leg and raise your right leg . Step towards the southeast with your right leg, circling the sword down and slightly up to your right. Touch your left toes forward on the ground, with your left

五、小魁星式（19圖）

五、小魁星式（左虛步撩）

抬右腿向東南上步，同時繞腕向東南提劍，劍尖朝斜下，同時左腳向東南上步成虛步，重心坐於右腿，左手配合，劍指點右腕。（圖19）

【注意】：

尾閭中正，虛實分清，含胸拔背。眼視前方，提劍時劍尖要朝斜下。

5 The Little Dipper

Sit on your left leg and raise your right leg . Step towards the southeast with your right leg, circling the sword down and slightly up to your right. Touch your left toes forward on the ground, with your left

20

六、燕子入巢（20-21圖）

leg empty. Center yourself on your right leg and sit. Left hand（two fingers）touches the right wrist（Fig 19）.

Points to notes：
- Look forward horizontally.
- word points diagonally downward.

六、燕子入巢（弓步直刺）

左腳抬起，以右腳前掌為軸，反轉 180 度。轉體時呈弧狀分臂，落左腳，雙手抱劍向西北斜下刺（圖 20-21）

【注意】：
尾閭中正，虛實分清，上下相隨，動作一致。轉體時

21

以腰為主，下刺時雙臂忌直，應當呈弧形。

6 Swallow Returns To The Nest

Turn your body 180 degrees to your left by pivoting on the ball of your right foot, at the same time raising your left leg. As you turn your body, you should open your arms and circle them back（Fig 20）.

As you step forward into a bow stance with your left leg you should join your hands to hold the sword with both hands, then pierce diagonally downwards to the northwest（Fig 21）.

Points to notes：

● Coordinate hand and leg movements.

● Turn your waist to the left as you pivot on the ball of your right foot.

● Arms should not be straight but rounded with elbow slightly bent.

22

七、靈貓捕鼠（22-25 圖）

七、靈貓捕鼠（墊步前躍下刺）

1. 左腳腳尖抬起向左轉 45 度，同時右腳提膝，腳尖自然下垂，雙手回縮，下帶劍柄，此時劍尖上挑。

2. 下坐左腿，右腳上步，落地彈跳，彈跳時，劍隨體動呈波浪形，落地後成弓步，落地時，左手從側面畫弧上撩，劍指上翹，右手握劍向西北斜下刺，眼視方向和劍尖一致。（圖 22-25）

【注意】：

尾閭中正，含胸拔背，動作連貫。彈跳時輕鬆自然，落地穩健。左手上撩時注意垂肘，右手握劍要對地斜下刺，忌直，要保持弧形。

23   24

7 Spirrited Cat Catches The Mouse

Pivot 45 degrees on your left heel. Raise your right knee, toes pointing down naturally. Using both hands, withdraw the sword slightly to point diagonally upwards (Fig 22) .

Sit on your left leg. Step forward with your right leg (Fig 23) .

Raise your left leg and prepare to jump (Fig 24) .

Jump onto your left leg and step forward into a bow stance with your right leg. Letting go of the sword with your left hand, circle your left hand (two fingers) upward and forward. With your right hand, pierce diagonally downwards with the sword to the northwest. Look in the direction of the sword. As you jump, raise and lower the sword in a wavelike motion. (Fig 25) .

嫡傳楊家太極劍

25

Points to notes：

- Hands and legs move in concordance without pausing.
- Jump naturally in a relaxed manner.
- aintain a steady balance at all times.
- Lelax your left arm with its elbow pointing downward .
- Keep your right arm rounded when piercing with the sword.

26

八、鳳凰抬頭（26 圖）

八、鳳凰抬頭（弓步平跳）

左手劍指下落直指右腕，同時配合右手屈腕挑劍，劍尖朝右斜上。（圖 26）

【注意】：

雙手配合協調，眼神和劍尖所指方向一致，注意雙臂呈弧形，挑劍時注意垂肘。

8 Phoenix Raises Its Head

Move your left hand down towards your right wrist. Simultaneously, using a wrist action, raise the point of the sword to point diagonally upward（Fig 26）.

27   28

九、黃蜂入洞（27–31 圖）

Points to notes：

● Coordinate left and right hand movements.
● Look in the direction of the sword.
● Keep arms rounded, rather than straight.
● Light elbow points downward.

九、黃蜂入洞（轉身下刺）

1. 屈腕劍指西南，同時右腿以腳跟為軸向南 90 度，坐右腿，劍指正南。

2. 抬左腿腳跟著地，腳尖向東北，左手成弧狀隨腰轉動。抬右腳腳跟落地，腳尖指向北方。抬左腿向前上步成弓步，同時雙臂呈弧狀開、合，向西北斜下刺。（圖 27–31）

29   30

【注意】：

　　動作以腰為主，尾閭中正，含胸拔背，上下相隨，配合協調。注意轉體動作自始而終為 360 度，目光和劍尖所指方向一致。

9　Yellow Bee Enters The Hive

Circle your right hand towards the southwest to turn the edge of the sword southwards, the sword to be positioned horizontally in front of your chest. Simultaneously, turn 90 degrees on your right heel and sit on your right leg（Fig 26）.

Turn your waist to the left（Fig 27）.

Points to notes：
- Look in the direction of the sword.

31

Raise your left leg and step on to its heel, pivoting the left foot on its heel to point its toes to the northeast. Circle your left hand to the left to follow the turning of the waist（Fig 28）.

Raise your right leg and step on to its heel, pivoting the right foot on its heel to point its toes to the north. Open your arms by circling your hands backwards（Fig 29）.

Sit on your right leg and raise the left leg（Fig 30）.

Step into a bow stance with your left leg towards the northwest. Hold the sword with both hands and pierce downwards（Fig 31）.

Points to notes：

- Keep your waist centered.
- Coordinate hand and leg movements.
- Turn 360 degrees.
- Look in the direction of the sword.

十、鳳凰右展翅（32-33 圖）

十、鳳凰右展翅（弓步右掃）

轉腕劍指正西，同時左腳以腳跟為軸向東北轉 90 度，左手劍指點右腕，抬右腿同時轉腰向東南上步成弓步，兩臂呈弧形漸漸分開，劍向東南斜上橫點，左手呈弧形，劍指向西北斜上翹。（圖 32–33）

【注意】：

動作以腰為主，橫點時兩手緊密配合，反刺橫點是個漸漸的過程。弓步忌「丁」字，點時注意垂肘。

33

10 Phoenlx Spreads Right Wing

Letting go of the sword with your left hand, circle your right wrist to point the sword westwards. At the same time, pivot 90 degrees on your left heel to point your left toes northeast. Left hand (two fingers) touches the right wrist (Fig 32) .

Raise your right leg, turn your waist towards the southeast, and step into a bow stance towards the southeast. Open your arms slowly in a circling motion to cut with the sword. Sword points diagonally upward to the southeast. Left hand (two fingers) circles toward the northwest as you cut with the sword (Fig 33) .

Points to notes :

• The correct turning of the waist is vital.

• Coordinate left and right hand movements to separate hem slowly.

• Bow stance should not be too narrow.

• Right elbow points downward in a relaxed manner.

嫡傳楊家太極劍

46

34

十一、小魁星（34-35 圖）

十一、小魁星（左虛步撩）

左腿後坐，抬右腿，腳尖下垂，同時劍柄向後繞圈，右腳向東南上步，提劍成虛步，左手配合，劍指點右腕。（圖 34-35）

【注意】：

尾閭中正，虛實分清，含胸拔背，動作連貫協調。提劍時注意垂肘，虛步時腳尖點地。

35

11 The Little Dipper

Sit on your left leg. Raise your right leg with the toes pointing down. Circle the sword backwards towards your left. Step forward with the right foot, toes pointing southeast. Circle the sword slightly up to the right. Place the left toes forward on the ground, keeping the left leg empty. Left hand (two fingers) follows right hand to touch at the wrist (Fig 34–35).

Points to notes :
- Do not pause in the middle of the movement.
- Seek concordance and smooth continuity in your movements.
- Right elbow relaxes to point down.
- Left leg remains empty with toes touching lightly on the ground.

36

十二、鳳凰左展翅（36圖）

十二、鳳凰左展翅（左弓步右點）

左腿向後移步，腳尖對正北方，兩臂分開，左手向西北後撩，右手向東南微開。（圖36）

12　Phoenix Spreads Left Wing

Step back with your left leg, with your left toes pointing north. At the same time, open your arms. As you open your arms, your right hand moves the sword in a southeasterly direction with its blade pointing diagonally downward. Your left hand（two fingers）moves in a northwesterly direction, lifting lightly（Fig 36）.

Points to notes：

● Seek concordance in arm and leg movements.

37

十三、等魚勢（37-38 圖）

十三、等魚勢（虛步點劍）

劍自右向左畫弧反點，左手劍指配合指向劍柄後端。右腳回縮，面向正東成虛步。（圖 37-38）

【注意】：

眼隨劍身轉動，轉時以腰為主，尾閭中正，虛實分清，動作協調，劍柄正對腋下劍尖指向正南。

38

13 Waiting For The Fish

Turn the sword around to cut downwards with the heart of the right hand facing upwards. Left hand (two fingers) follows the sword to point at the hilt. Raise your right leg, move it back, then forward to touch the toes lightly on the ground. The right leg is empty (Figures 37 – 38).

Points to notes :
- The eyes follow the turning of the sword.
- The turning of the waist is vital.

39

十四、左右龍行式（39-41 圖）

十四、左右龍行式（左右前刺）

　　1. 收右腿後坐，微向東南上步成弓步，同時帶劍回縮，翻劍向東北斜刺（微斜）。

　　2. 上左腿向東北成弓步，劍柄回縮，翻劍向東南斜刺（微斜）。

　　3. 上右腿向東南成弓步，劍柄回縮，翻劍向東北斜刺（微斜）。（圖 39-41）

　　【注意】：

　　動作以腰為主，上下相隨，尾閭中正，動作協調，弓步忌「丁」字。目光與劍尖所指方向一致。左手配合要協調。

40

14 Dragon Goes Left And Right

Raise your right leg, bring it back, then step forward into a bow stance, toes pointing southeast. Withdraw the sword to your right, then pierce towards the east and slightly north. The heart of the right hand faces downward. Left hand（two ingers）touches the right wrist（Fig 39）.

Step forward with your left leg into a bow stance, toes pointing northeast. Turn the heart of your right hand up and pierce with the sword toward the east and slightly south（Fig 40）.

Step forward with your right leg into a bow stance, toes pointing southeast. Turn the heart of your right hand down and pierce with the sword toward the east and slightly north（Fig 41）.

41

Points to notes：
- Bow stance must not be too narrow.
- Look towards where the sword points.
- Left and right hands move in concordance.

十五、宿鳥投林（獨立上刺）

　　1. 抬左腿，同時左手後撩繞圈和後縮劍柄匯合。坐左腿，提右腿，腳尖點地成虛步，劍尖斜向上，目光注視劍鋒。

　　2. 坐左腿，右腿微收，劍柄後撤，左手配合，劍指點右腕，然後上右腿，左腿提膝，腳尖自然下垂，左手配合右手舉劍斜向上刺。

42

十五、宿鳥投林（42-44 圖）

【注意】：

尾閭中正，含胸拔背，上下相隨，動作協調，獨立時立地要穩，眼視劍尖。（圖 42-44）

15　Bird Returns To The Wood

Raise your left leg and circle your left hand（two fingers）back（Fig 42）.

Next, sit on your left leg and raise your right leg. Place your right toes forward lightly on the ground, right leg remaining empty. At the same time, bring the sword and the left hand（two fingers）towards each other. The sword points diagonally upwards. Look in the direction of the sword.

Sit on your left leg while drawing back your right leg and the sword simultaneously. Left hand（two fingers）touches the hilt of the sword（Fig 43）.

43　　　　　　　　44

Step forward with your right leg. Raise your left knee, toes pointing downward naturally. Pierce diagonally upwards with the sword,
balancing independently on one leg. Left hand（two fingers）follows
the right hand（Fig 44）.

Points to notes：

● Maintain a steady balance on one leg.

十六、烏龍擺尾（虛步下戳）

左腳跟著地，腳尖朝東北，重心坐左腳。右腳向東南
點地成虛步，同時兩臂分開，劍自左方畫弧下點，左手配
合左上撩起。（圖45）

45

十六、烏龍擺尾（45 圖）

【注意】：

尾閭中正，含胸拔背，虛實分清，動作協調。注意劍身與右臂成一條線，左手上撩注意垂肘。

16 Dragon Swings Its Tail

Place your left leg on the ground and sit on your left leg, toes pointing northeast. Circle the sword to your left and raise your right leg .

Place your right toes lightly on the ground towards the southeast. The right leg is empty. At the same time circle the sword to your right. Sword points diagonally downwards to your right. Left hand（two fingers）circles to your left and up（Fig 45）.

Points to notes：

- Right arm is straight, in line with the sword（Fig 45）.
- Left elbow points downward.

十七、青龍出水（46圖）

十七、青龍出水（左弓步刺）

收右腿上步，右手抬劍從體前繞圈，左手畫弧上撩，左腿向東北上步成弓步，翻腕抬劍，向東北斜上刺。（圖46）

【注意】：

動作以腰為主，尾閭中正，含胸拔背，動作協調，左手上撩時注意垂肘，弓步忌「丁」字。

17 Dragon Emerges From Water

Raise your right leg backwards, then step forward and sit on your right leg. Step into a bow stance with the left leg, its toes pointing to the northeast. Turn the heart of your right hand upwards and pierce diagonally upwards to the northeast with the sword. Left hand (two fingers) circles upwards (Fig 46) .

Points to notes :
- Waist movement is vital.
- Left elbow points downward.

47

十八、風捲荷葉（47–48 圖）

十八、風捲荷葉（轉身斜帶）

1. 左腳以腳跟為軸向南轉 90 度，左手點右腕，右手握劍繞腕。

2. 抬右腳向正西方轉體落地，握劍向前平推，同時後腳抬起後蹬成弓步。（圖 47–48）

【注意】：

整個動作以腰為主。尾閭中正，虛實分清，推劍和後蹬動作一致。

48

18 Lotus Leaf Blown By The Wind

Pivot 90 degrees or more on your left heel to point your left toes to the south. At the same time, turn the sword to the left using a wrist movement. Left hand (two fingers) touches right wrist.

Raise your right leg and turn your body to the west. Place your right foot on the ground. Raise your left leg and step backwards into a bow stance while pushing the sword forward (Fig 47–48) .

Points to notes :

- Waist movement is vital.
- Move the sword forward and the left leg backwards simultaneously.

49　50

十九、左右獅子搖頭（49–52圖）

十九、左右獅子搖頭（退步左右橫掃）

1. 坐左腿同時繞腕，重心左移。
2. 退右腿同時繞腕，重心右坐。
3. 退左腿同時繞腕，重心左坐。
4. 退右腿同時繞腕，重心右坐。（圖49–52）

【注意】：
尾閭中正，含胸拔背，動作靈活，步法穩健，虛實分清，目隨劍行。

51   52

19 Lion Shakes Its Head Left & Right

Sit on your left leg and center yourself on your left leg. At the same time, turn the sword to your left using a wrist movement .

Step backwards with your right leg and center yourself on your right leg. At the same time, turn the sword to your right using a wrist movement.

Step backwards with your left leg and center yourself on your left leg. At the same time, turn the sword to your left using a wrist movement (Fig 49–52) .

Points to notes :

- Keep your movements circular and relaxed.
- Clearly differentiate between solid and empty.
- Follow the sword with your eyes.

53

二十、虎抱頭（53-54 圖）

二十、虎抱頭（提膝捧劍）

　　承上勢，兩臂呈弧形分開，同時左腿微抬，落地重心移於左腿，右腿提膝，雙手捧劍，成獨立式。（圖53-54）

　　【注意】：
　　尾閭中正，動作協調，上下相隨，獨立時立地穩健，目隨劍行。

54

20 Tiger Holds Its Head

Step backwards with your right leg and open your arms. Raise your left knee slightly .

Place your left foot on the ground and center yourself on your left leg. Raise your right knee until it points slightly upwards. Hold the sword with both hands while standing independently on one leg (Figures 53 & 54).

Points to notes :
- Maintain a steady balance on one leg.
- Follow the sword with your eyes.

55　　　　56

二十一、野馬跳澗（55–57 圖）

二十一、野馬跳澗（墊步前遠跳下刺）

　　下坐左腿，右腿向前上步，彈起遠跳，跳起雙手握劍成波浪形擺動，落地後成弓步，握劍平下刺。（圖55–57）

66

　　【注意】：
　　動作基本要求與「靈貓撲鼠」大致相同，不同的是落地後彈跳要跳得遠，握劍應注意平下刺。

57

21 Wild Horse Jumps Over River

Sit on your left leg and step forward with your right leg (Fig 55).
Raise your left leg and prepare to jump (Fig 56).

Jump on to your left leg, then step into a bow stance with the right leg. As you jump, move the sword up and down in a wavelike motion, then pierce downwards as you step into the bow stance (Fig 57).

Points to notes :
- Do a long jump, not a high jump.

58

二十二、勒馬式（58-59 圖）

二十二、勒馬式（右側背劍式）

　　右腳以腳跟為軸按順時針方向轉體 180 度，同時左腳左移成虛步，雙手握劍自右肩外側上繞向前平擺。（圖58-59）

　　【注意】：
　　動作連貫，尾閭中正，配合協調，背劍時不要貼體，而應從右臂右上方繞過。

59

22 Rein In The Horse

Pivot 90 degrees on your right heel as you turn your waist 180 degrees to your left. Draw the sword over your shoulder, not directly over, but a little to the side (Fig 58).

Raise your left leg, then place it lightly on the ground. Raise the point of the sword as it passes over your shoulder, then point the sword forward. Place your left toes lightly on the ground (Fig 59).

Points to notes :
- Seek concordance in arm and leg movements.
- The sword must not touch your shoulder.

60

二十三、指南針（60 圖）

二十三、指南針（弓步直刺）

收左腿，同時劍向右側回帶，左腳上步，右腳跟上，成平行開立式，雙手握劍前刺。（圖 60）

【注意】：

尾閭中正，含胸拔背，虛實分清，開立時兩腳平行，與肩等寬。雙手握劍成弧形。

23 Compass

Raise your left leg backwards. At the same time, draw back the sword（Fig 64）.

Step forward with your left leg, followed by your right leg, to stand with feet a shoulder-width apart. Using both hands, pierce forward with the sword（Fig 65）.

61   62

二十四、左右迎風撣塵（61-66 圖）

Points to notes：

- Feet must be a shoulder-width apart.

二十四、左右迎風撣塵（左右弓步攔點）

1. 重心右坐，右腿半蹲，以腳跟為軸向東南轉 45 度，左腿提膝，腳尖自然下垂，同時劍向右帶，左手配合，劍指點右腕。左腿向東北上步成弓步，繞腕向東北斜上點劍。

2. 上右腿成弓步，繞腕向東南斜上點劍。

3. 上左腿成弓步，繞腕向東北斜上點劍。（圖 61-66）

63   64

【注意】：

尾閭中正，含胸拔背，動作協調，虛實分清，眼隨劍影，點劍時注意垂肘，左手配合協調。

24 Dusting In The Wind, Left And Right

Sit a little on your right leg as you pivot 45 degrees on your right heel. At the same time, draw back the sword（Fig 61）.

Step into a bow stance to the northeast with your left leg. At the same time, cut with the sword to the northeast（Fig 62）.

Draw back the sword to your left, step into a bow stance to the southeast with your right leg, and cut with the sword to the southeast（Figures 63 – 64）.

Draw back the sword to your right, step into a bow stance to the northeast with your left leg and cut with the sword to the northeast（Figures 65– 66）

65　　　　　　　　　　　　66

Points to notes：

- Follow the sword with your eyes.
- Left hand（two fingers）moves in concordance with the right hand.

67

68

二十五、順水推舟（67–70 圖）

二十五、順水推舟（進步反刺）

1. 左腳以腳跟為軸按順時針方向旋轉，抬右腿向西北上步成弓步，繃腕挑劍，左手配合點腕。

2. 轉右腳跟，提肘轉腕劍尖朝上畫弧至斜下，收左腿然後向前上步成弓步，向前推劍。左手配合點腕。（圖67–70）

【注意】：

尾閭中正，含胸拔背，動作協調，虛實分清，腰腿配合協調，動作一致。

70

25 Push The Boat To Follow The Current

Pivot on your left heel

Raise your right leg and step into a bow stance to the northwes. Circle the sword towards the northewst using a wrist movement to lower and raise the sword .

Step into a bow stance to the southeast while pushing forward with the sword. Left hand (two fingers) touches your right wrist (Fig 67–70) .

Points to notes :

• Seek concordance between waist and leg movements.

71

二十六、流星趕月（71圖）

二十六、流星趕月（反身回點）

　　左腳以腳跟為軸向西南旋轉，收右腿向西北上步成弓步，同時分臂，畫弧分劍向西北斜下點劍，左手配合，劍指後點。（圖71）

　　【注意】：
　　動作以腰為主，尾閭中正，含胸拔背，虛實分清，動作協調，左手劍指後點時注意垂肘。

26 Shooting Star Chases The Moon

Pivot on your left heel and raise your right leg (Fig 76) .

Step forward into a bow stance facing northwest. As you move into the bo stance, move your hands apart in an arc to cut downward. The sword points diagonally downwards to the northwest. The back-ward movement of the left hand (two fingers) reinforces the forward movement of the sword (Fig 71) .

Points to note :

• Your left elbow points downwards in a relaxed manner as you hold up the two fingers of your left hand.

72

二十七、天馬飛瀑（72圖）

二十七、天馬飛瀑（虛步點劍）

抬左腿向東南換步，右腿向南上步成虛步，同時提劍畫弧向南斜下點劍，左手配合，劍指點於右腕。（圖72）

【注意】：

尾閭中正，含胸拔背，動作協調，虛實分清，眼神腰腿左右手配合一致。

27 Heavenly Steed Flies Over Waterfall

Raise your left leg and step to the southeast .

Raise your left leg and place its toes lightly down towards the south, the right leg remaining empty. Turn the sword using a wrist movement to cut diagonally downwards to the south. Left hand (two fingers) follows the right hand to touch the right wrist (Fig 72) .

Points to note :

• Eyes, waist, left hand and right hand work in concordance to effect the sword movement.

73

二十八、挑簾式（73-74 圖）

二十八、挑簾式（獨立平托）

右手向左繞腕（劍尖朝東）。向右轉體，右腳腳尖向西北落地。同時左腿提膝，腳尖自然下垂，成獨立式，右手畫弧向上舉劍，左手配合，劍指點於右腕。（圖73-74）

【注意】：

轉體以腰為主，動作協調，虛實分清，含胸拔背，尾閭中正，挑簾時注意左腿下坐，舉劍時劍尖微向斜上（指向正南），挑簾式雙手都應注意垂肘。

74

28 Raise The Curtain

Circle the sword leftwards to point east

Turn your body to the right and step with your right leg towards
the northwest .

Raise your left knee, toes pointing downward naturally. Circle the
sword to your right and raise it to point forward and slightly upward.
Left hand（two fingers）follows your right hand.

Points to note：

- Sit on your left leg as you circle the sword to your left.
- Sword points slightly upward from the horizontal（Fig 73–74）.
- Keep both elbows relaxed and pointing downward.

81

75

二十九、左右車輪（75-76 圖）

二十九、左右車輪（左右輪掃，弓步前點）

　　左腳向左側落地，右腳向前上步成弓步，右手和左手交叉繞圈，右手向西斜下點劍，左手劍指合併成弧形後點。（圖 75-76）

　　【注意】：
　　尾閭中正，含胸拔背，虛實分清，上下相隨，點劍應注意向斜下，弓步忌「丁」字，左手劍指後點注意垂肘。

76

29 Left And Right Wheels

Step forward with your left leg. Circle the sword down to your left .
Step forward with your right leg .

Begin to raise the sword as you begin to shift your weight forward into a bow stance .

Circle the sword forward and down to point diagonally downwards to the west. At the same time, your left hand (two fingers) circles back and down (Fig 75-76) .

Points to note :

• Hands move in coordination to reinforce sword movement.
• Sword points diagonally downwards.
• Left elbow relaxes to point downwards.

77   78

三十、燕子銜泥（77-79 圖）

三十、燕子銜泥（虛步點劍）

退右腿左手合劍，抬左腿分劍，落左腳，上右腿，腳尖點地成虛步，左手合劍向西斜下方點劍。（圖77-79）

【注意】：

尾閭中正，含胸拔背，動作協調，上下相隨，左右手配合緊密。

79

30 Swallow Picks Up Mud

Step back with your right leg as you bring your left hand (two fingers) towards the sword (Fig 77) .

Separate your hands, then step forward with your left leg (Fig 78) .

Sitting on your left leg, touch your right toes lightly forward on the ground. Circle the sword forward to point diagonally downwards towards the west. Left hand (two fingers) is brought towards the right at the same time (Fig 79) .

Points to note :

- Synchronise the raising and lowering of the hands.
- The coordination of left and right hand movements reinforces the sword movement.

80

三十一、大鵬展翅（80-81 圖）

三十一、大鵬展翅（撤步右橫掃）

右手向左繞腕，劍尖朝南，收右腿向東北上步成弓步，同時握劍自胸前畫弧，漸漸翻劍，向東北斜上橫點，左手配合後分。（圖 80-81）

【注意】：

動作協調，上下相隨，尾閭中正，含胸拔背，左手上撩時注意垂肘，成弓步時左腳跟抬起後移，注意眼神。

81

31 Gigantic Bird (ROC) Spreads Its Wings

Turning the sword to the south using a wrist movement (Fig 80).

Raise your right leg and step into a bow stance to the northeast, pivoting your left foot on its toes. At the same time, turn the sword slowly to the northeast at chest level. Sword points diagonally upward. Left hand (two ingers) moves back as right hand moves forward (Fig 81).

Points to note :

• Raise your left heel to pivot on toes.

• Left hand (two fingers) circles backwards in concordance with right hand circling forward (Fig 81).

87

三十二、海底撈月（82-84圖）

三十二、海底撈月（右弓步撩）

向左轉右腳跟，右手向左翻腕，左手劍指點右腕。劍尖朝上，收左腿向前上步，落地後右腳向前上步成弓步，同時繞腕弧形向前撩劍，左手向後畫劍。劍指上撩。（圖82-84）

【注意】：

動作以腰為主，尾閭中正，含胸拔背，上下相隨，動作協調。向前撩時注意手心向上。

84

32 Raise The Moon From The Sea-Bed

Pivoting on your right heel, point the sword upwards by lowering your right wrist. At the same time, touch your right wrist with your left hand (two fingers).

Raise and withdraw your left leg.

Step forward onto the left leg Step forward into a bow stance with your right leg. At the same time, circle the sword forward in a lifting motion. The left hand (two fingers) circles to the left and back (Fig 82-84).

Points to note :

• The heart of your right hand faces up as it is circling the sword forward.

85

三十三、懷中抱月（85圖）

三十三、懷中抱月（退步拖劍）

抬左腳，落地後重心左坐，隨之抬右腿腳尖點地成虛步，合劍懷抱。（圖85）

【注意】：

動作以腰為主，虛實分清，上下相隨，尾閭中正，含胸拔背，懷中抱月時，劍尖朝斜上。

33 Cradle The Moon Against Your Chest

Sit on your right leg and raise your left leg（Fig 85）. Placing your left foot behind your right foot, sit on your left leg. Raise your right leg and touch the toes forward（empty）. Sword points diagonally up. Left hand（two fingers）touches the sword hilt.

86

三十四、哪吒探海（86圖）

三十四、哪吒探海（獨立下刺）

收右腿向前上步，重心右移，同時右手握劍向回微縮。左腿提膝，腳尖下垂，右手握劍向斜下刺，左手配合畫弧上撩，成獨立式。（圖86）

【注意】：

動作以腰為主，尾閭中正，虛實分清，上下相隨，配合緊密，下刺時握劍為掌心向上。

34 Boy Buddha Looks In The Sea

Raise and withdraw your right leg. At the same time, withdraw the sword slightly.

87

三十五、犀牛望月（87圖）

Stepping forward, change your center to the right leg. Raise your left knee, toes pointing downwards naturally. At the same time, pierce diagonally downwards with the sword. Circle your left hand forward as you pierce with the right. Maintain an independent balance on one leg (Fig 86).

Points to note：

● The heart of your right hand faces up.

三十五、犀牛望月（弓步平托劍）

左手自上而下繞圈，右手抬劍，雙手合劍，同時左腿向東上步成弓步，此時劍尖朝西，眼神與劍尖方向一致。（圖87）

【注意】：

尾閭中正，含胸拔背，動作協調，上下相隨，眼神與劍尖方向一致，注意垂肘。

35 Rhinoceros Admires The Moon

Circle your left hand（two fingers）around to meet your right hand as it pull the sword back in a circular movement to point westward. At the same time, step to the east with your left leg. Look in the direction of the sword（Fig 87）.

Points to note：

- Look in the direction at which the sword points.
- Elbow points downwards.

88

三十六、射雁式（88 圖）

三十六、射雁式（虛步回抽）

抬右腿上步，重心右坐，左腿向東南點步成虛步，同時右手握劍繞腕。畫弧至胯下，左手繞圈呈弧形前指。（圖88）

【注意】：
動作以腰為主，尾閭中正，含胸拔背，虛實分清，動作協調。劍到胯下應為劍尖朝斜下，眼望劍尖方向。

36 Shooting Wild Geese

Raise your right leg and step forward to the southeast. Raise your left leg and touch the toes gently forward（empty）. Circle the sword

89

三十七、青龍現爪（89 圖）

forward and back to the rest at waist level. Left hand（two fingers）circles forward Sword points diagonally up towards the southeast.（Fig 88）

Points to note：
- Look towards where the sword points.

三十七、青龍現爪（跟步平刺）

抬左腿上步，右腳跟步，與左腳平行，面向東南，同時雙手畫弧，向東南前刺。（圖89）

【注意】：
尾閭中正，含胸拔背，動作協調，上下相隨，平行站立時與肩等寬，前刺時注意劍尖向上微斜。

90

三十八、鳳凰雙展翅（90–91 圖）

37 Dragon Shows Its Claws

Raise your left leg and step forward, followed by the right leg to
stand facing southeast. At the same time, open your arms, then join
your hands to pierce with the sword towards the southeast（Fig 89）.

Points to note：
● Sword points slightly upwards.

三十八、鳳凰雙展翅（左右橫掃）

左腳以腳跟為軸按順時針方向轉腳尖，右腳向西北上
步成弓步，同時繞腕翻劍，漸漸向西北斜上畫弧橫點。左
手配合後撩。（圖90–91）

91

38 Phoenix Spreads Its Wings

Pivoting on your left heel, raise your right leg and step to the northwest in a bow stance. Using a wrist action, circle the sword back andorward to point diagonally up towards the northwest. Left hand (two fingers) moves in the opposite direction to the right hand (Figures 90–91).

Points to note :
● Keep your body straight.
● Left hand reinforces the sword movement by moving backwards as the sword moves forwards.

92

三十九、左右跨攔（92-94圖）

三十九、左右跨攔（左右平托劍）

1. 右手繞腕，左手劍指點右腕，同時左腳向西南上步成弓步，此時握劍平放，手心向左，劍尖指向北方。（圖92-94）

【注意】：

尾閭中正，含胸拔背，動作協調，繞腕時劍尖朝下，目光向前遠視，弓步忌「丁」字步。

93   94

39 Stride Over The Hurdle

Turn down the point of the sword（Fig 92）.

Raise your left leg and step to the southwest into a bow stance. The sword points north as you move your right hand to your left, the heart of the right hand facing towards you. Left hand（two fingers）touches right wrist（Fig 93）.

Circle the right hand to point the sword to the south, with the heart of the right hand facing away from you. At the same time, step to the northwest in a bow stance with your right leg（Fig 94）.

Points to note :

• Begin by turning the point of the sword down, then circling your right hand to the right hand to the left（Figures 92– 94）.

• Look into the distance.

95

四十、射雁式（95圖）

四十、射雁式（虛步回抽）

後退右腳並下坐，重心右移，左腳向前。腳尖點地成虛步，右手握劍繞圈至右側胯下。（圖95）

【注意】：

尾閭中正，含胸拔背，上下相隨，動作協調，目光與左手劍指方向一致。

40 Shooting Wild Geese

Step back with your right leg and change your center to your right leg. Raise your left leg and place the toes gently forward（empty）. Circle the sword forward and back to rest at waist level. Left hand

96

四十一、白猿獻果（96圖）

（two fingers）circles forward. Sword points diagonally up towards the northwest（Fig95）.

Points to note：
● Look towards where the sword points.

四十一、白猿獻果（虛步橫點劍）

左腳向南移步，面轉西，右腳向西上步，腳尖點地成虛步。同時雙手分合，橫點托劍，面向正西，劍尖平指西方。（圖96）

【注意】：

尾閭中正，含胸拔背，虛實分清，上下相隨，動作協調。托劍時劍身略高於肩。

97

四十二、左右落花（97–101 圖）

41 White Monkey Presents Fruit

Step towards the southwest with your left leg as you turn towards the west, opening your arms . Place your right toes gently forward towards the west（right leg empty）. At the same time bring your hands together to hold the sword pointing horizontally westward（Fig 96）.

Points to note：
● The sword is held slightly above shoulder height.

四十二、左右落花（左右退掃）

1. 左手劍指點右腕，配合右手繞腕。同時坐左腿，後退右腿。（圖 97）

98   99

2. 坐右腿，重心右移退左腿，同時雙手配合，握劍繞圈。（圖98）

3. 坐左腿，重心左移退右腿，同時左手劍指點右腕，配合右手握劍繞圈。（圖99）

4. 坐右腿，重心右移退左腿。同時左手劍指點右腕，配合右手握劍繞圈。（圖100）

5. 坐左腿，重心左移退右腿，同時左手劍指點右腕，配合右手握劍繞圈。（圖101）

【注意】：

動作以腰為主，尾閭中正，動作協調，上下相隨，虛實分清，特別應注意後退時重心越坐越低（動作一個比一個要低）。

100　　　　　　　　　101

42　A Flower Falls, Left And Right

Touch your right wrist with your left hand（two fingers）. Circle your right hand leftwards as you sit on your left leg（Fig 97）.

Step backwards with your right leg. Sit on your right leg. Move your right hand to the right.（Fig 97）.

Step backwards with your left leg. Sit on your left leg. Move your right hand to the left（Fig 98）.

Step backwards with your right leg. Sit on your right leg. Move your right hand to the right（Fig 99）.

Step backwards with your left leg. Sit on your left leg. Move your right hand to the left（Fig 100）.

Step backwards with your right leg. Sit on your right leg. Move your right hand to the right（Fig 101）.

Points to note：

● Sit lower with each step.

102　　　　　　　　　　103

四十三、玉女穿梭（102-103 圖）

四十三、玉女穿梭（斜身弓步下刺）

收左腿向南上步成弓步，同時繞腕向南斜下刺，左手畫弧上撩。（圖 102-103）

【注意】：
動作協調，上下相隨，弓步忌「丁」字，上撩時注意垂肘。

43 Fair Lady Works The Shuttle

Step into a bow stance towards the south with your left leg. At the same time, pierce diagonally downwards with the sword towards the south. Left hand（two fingers）circles upwards（Figures 102 – 103）.

104

四十四、白虎攪尾（104-105 圖）

Points to note：

● Left elbow relaxes to point down.

四十四、白虎攪尾（轉身上挑）

1. 左腳以腳跟為軸右轉，坐左腿，同時右手轉腕，左手點腕，手心向右，劍尖平指東方。（圖 104）

2. 抬右腳向北上步，轉身成弓步，同時右手握劍，劍尖朝下畫弧，向上挑劍。（圖 105）

【注意】：

動作以腰為主，尾閭中正，動作協調，上下相隨，含胸拔背，定勢後劍尖朝上，眼視前方。

105

44 White Tiger Swings Its Tail

Pivot on your left heel and sit on your left leg. At the same time, turn the sword to the left with a wrist action. Left hand（two fingers）touches the right wrist（Fig 104）.

Step to the north with right leg into a bow stance. Circle the sword towards the north, raise it with a wrist action to point upwards（Fig 105）.

Points to note：
• The sword is vertical.

四十五、魚跳龍門（106–111 圖）

四十五、魚跳龍門（墊步上跳前下刺）

1. 抬左腿微向西上步（腳尖朝西南），同時兩臂分開，右腿提膝，腳尖自然下垂，合手抱劍成獨立式。（圖106）

2. 左腿下坐，劍向回縮，右腳上步，落地向上彈跳，彈跳時劍成波浪形擺動，落地成弓步，雙手抱劍前刺。（圖107–111）

【注意】：

尾閭中正，動作協調，含胸拔背，上下相隨。落地彈跳要高，區別靈貓撲鼠（朝下）和野馬跳澗（向前）。

107

45 Fish Jumps Over The Dragon Gate

Raise your left leg and step westward with the toes pointing southwest. Open your arms. Raise your right knee, toes pointing downward naturally. Hold the sword with both hands. Balance independently on one leg.

Sit on your left leg.

Withdraw the sword slightly. Place your right foot forward gently on the ground.

Chang your center to your right leg. Raise your left leg and prepare to jump.

Jump forward onto your left leg then step into a bow stance with your right leg. As you jump, raise and lower the sword in a wavelike movement. As you step into a bow stance, pierce forward and down using both hands (Fig 106-111).

108

110

109

Points to note：
- Jump high rather than far.

110

111

112   113

四十六、左右烏龍絞柱（112-114圖）

四十六、左右烏龍絞柱（左絞掃、右絞點）

後坐左腿，左手劍指點右腕，右手抬劍向左繞圈，同時收右腿向前上步，腳尖向西北。隨之左腳向西上步，轉體坐右腿，反腕向東北斜點。同時左手後分。（圖112-114）

【注意】：

動作以腰為主，尾閭中正，虛實分清，上下相隨，動作協調，眼視劍尖。劍尖指向東北斜下，後撩時注意垂肘，劍指上翹。

114

46 Dragon Wraps Around Pillar

Sit on your left leg. Touch your right wrist with your left hand (two fingers). Circle the sword leftwards. Raise your right leg and step towards the northeast. Raise your left leg and step back towards the west. At the same time, sit on your right leg, turn your body to face northeast and circle the sword rightwards to point diagonally down-wards towards the northeast. Left hand (two fingers) circles back (Fig 112–114).

Points to note :

- Look in the direction of the sword.
- The sword points diagonally downwards towards the northeast.
- Left hand (two fingers) points up.

115

四十七、仙人指路（115–116 圖）

四十七、仙人指路（弓步斜下刺）

左手和左腿同時後收，左腿上步，左手繞圈上撩（重心左移），右腳上步成弓步。同時右手握劍繞圈，轉體向西前刺。（圖 115–116）

【注意】：

動作以腰為主，尾閭中正，含胸拔背，上下相隨，動作協調。前刺時手心向上，後撩時注意垂肘。

116

47 Fairy Shows The Way

Circle your left hand (two fingers) rightwards towards the sword. At the same time raise your left leg (Fig 115) .

Taking two steps towards the west, step into a bow stance with the right leg forward. Turning your body to the left, pierce forward with the sword. At the same time, circle your left hand (two fingers) back (Fig 116) .

Points to note :
• The heart of your right hand faces upwards.

117

四十八、朝天一柱香（117-118 圖）

四十八、 朝天一柱香（弓步豎劍）

右腳以腳跟為軸按順時針方向旋轉，左手自上而下繞圈上撩，收右腿向東上步成弓步，面朝南方，同時右手抬劍，劍尖朝上向右畫弧與左手匯合，左手劍指點右腕。此時劍尖朝上，手心向裏，劍身倒豎。（圖 117-118）

【注意】：

動作以腰為主，尾閭中正，含胸拔背，動作協調，上下相隨，注意定勢時劍身偏在身體左側，注意垂肘。

118

48 Worship The Sky With One Incense Stick

Pivot on your right heel, raise your left leg and step towards the east into a bow stance (Fig 117).

At the same time, circle your left hand (two fingers) to touch your right wrist. The sword points upwards vertically. The heart of the right hand faces towards you (Fig 118).

Points to note :

- The sword is positioned slightly to the left of center.
- Both elbows point downwards naturally.

119 120

四十九、風掃梅花（119-121 圖）

四十九、風掃梅花（旋轉平掃）

1. 左腳以腳跟為軸按順時針方向轉腳尖，同時向東轉腕，手心向下，劍尖朝東。（圖 119）

2. 收右腿隨之腳跟著地，重心右移，以右腳前掌為軸轉體 360 度，同時雙臂漸開。左腳落地，重心左移，右腳向前，腳尖點地成虛步，橫點抱劍。（圖 120-121）

【注意】：

動作以腰為主，尾閭中正，動作協調，轉體注意要旋轉 360 度，轉體同時兩臂漸開。

121

49 Wind Sweeps The Plum Flower

Pivot on your left heel. Turn the sword to point horizontally to the east. The heart of your right hand faces downwards .

Raise your right leg, step on to your right heel and pivot to your right .

Changing your center to your right leg, sweep your left leg around to the east and open your arms at the same time .

Changing your center to your left leg and place your right toes forward gently on the ground (empty) . Hold the sword with both hands to point forward (Fig 119–121) .

Points to note :
● Turn your body 360 degrees.
● As you turn, open your arms slowly.

119

122

五十、牙笏式（122-123圖）

五十、牙笏式（上步前上刺）

雙手回縮，同時收右腳上步，左腳跟上與右腳平行，腳尖向前，與肩等寬，抱劍前刺時劍尖微朝前上。（圖122-123）

123

50 Holding An Ivory Tablet

Withdraw the sword slightly as you withdraw your right leg（Fig 122）.

Step forward with your right leg, followed by your left leg to stand in a shoulder–width stance. Pierce forward with the sword using both hands（Fig 123）

Points to note：
- Your feet should be a shoulder–width apart.
- The sword should point slightly upwards.

124

五十一、抱劍歸原（124-126 圖）

五十一、抱劍歸原

剣交左手抱劍，繞圈還原。同時右手繞圈，右掌自然垂於身體右側，還原起勢。（圖 124-146）

【注意】：

尾閭中正，含胸拔背，眼視前方。動作協調，呼吸自然。腳尖向前，雙腳與肩等寬，平行，自然站立。

125

126

51 Return To The Start To Finish

Change the sword to your left hand（Fig 124）.

Hold out your hands, palms upwards（Fig 125）.

Circle both hands at 45 degrees and drop them to your sides, returning to the position at Fig 3（Fig 126）.

Points to note：

- Your toes should point straight ahead.
- Your feet should be a shoulder-width apart. Stand naturally.

導引養生功

1 疏筋壯骨功＋VCD
定價350元

2 導引保健功＋VCD
定價350元

3 頤身九段錦＋VCD
定價350元

4 九九還童功＋VCD
定價350元

5 舒心平血功＋VCD
定價350

6 益氣養肺功＋VCD
定價350元

7 養生太極扇＋VCD
定價350元

8 養生太極棒＋VCD
定價350元

9 導引養生形體詩韻＋VCD
定價350元

10 四十九式經絡動功＋VCD
定價350

張廣德養生著作　每冊定價350元

全系列為彩色圖解附教學光碟

輕鬆學武術

1 二十四式太極拳＋VCD
定價250元

2 四十二式太極拳＋VCD
定價250元

3 八式十六式太極拳＋VCD
定價250元

4 三十二式太極劍＋VCD
定價250元

5 四十二式太極劍＋VCD
定價250

6 二十八式木蘭拳＋VCD
定價250元

7 三十八式木蘭扇＋VCD
定價250元

8 四十八式木蘭劍＋VCD
定價250元

彩色圖解太極武術

1 太極功夫扇

定價220元

2 武當太極劍

定價220元

3 楊式太極劍56式

定價220元

4 楊式太極刀

定價220元

5 二十四式太極拳+VCD

定價350元

6 三十二式太極劍+VCD

定價350元

7 四十二式太極劍+VCD

定價350元

8 四十二式太極拳+VCD

定價350元

9 楊式十六式太極劍拳

定價350元

10 楊氏二十八式太極拳+VCD

定價350元

11 楊式太極拳四十式+VCD

定價350元

12 陳式太極拳五十六式+VCD

定價350元

13 吳式太極拳五十八式+VCD

定價350元

14 精簡陳式太極拳八式十六式

定價220元

15 精簡吳式太極拳三十六式 拳架‧推手

定價220元

16 夕陽美功夫扇

定價220元

17 綜合四十八式太極拳+VCD

定價350元

18 三十二式太極拳 四段

定價220元

19 楊式三十七式太極拳+VCD

定價350元

20 楊氏五十一式太極劍+VCD

定價350元

21 嫡傳楊家太極拳精練二十八式
定價220元

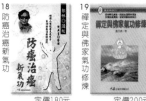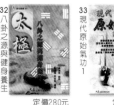

太極跤

1 太極防身術

定價300元

2 擒拿術

定價280元

3 中國式摔角

定價350元

簡化太極拳

1 陳式太極拳十三式

定價200元

2 楊式太極拳十三式

定價200元

3 吳式太極拳十三式

定價200元

4 武式太極拳十三式

定價200元

5 孫式太極拳十三式

定價200元

6 趙堡太極拳十三式

定價200元

原地太極拳

1 原地綜合太極二十四式

定價220元

2 原地活步太極四十二式

定價200元

3 原地簡化太極拳二十四式

定價200元

4 原地太極拳十二式

定價200元

5 原地青少年太極二十二式

定價220元

6 原地兒童太極拳十種十六式

定價180元

健康加油站

1 糖尿病預防與治療
定價200元

2 胃部機能與強健
定價180元

3 不孕症治療
定價200元

4 簡易醫學急救法
定價200元

5 肥胖健康診療
定價200元

6 肝功能健康診療
定價

7 高血壓健康診療
定價200元

8 高血糖健康診療
定價200元

9 尿酸值健康診療
定價200元

10 膽固醇中性脂肪健康診療
定價200元

11 痛風劇痛消除法
定價180元

12 三溫暖健康法
定價

13 手・腳病理按摩
定價180元

14 B型肝炎預防與治療
定價180元

15 吃得更漂亮、健康
定價180元

16 茶使您更健康
定價180元

17 圖解常見疾病運動療法
定價180元

18 科學健身改變亞健康
定價

19 簡易萬病自療保健
定價220元

20 王朝秘藥媚酒
定價180元

21 立見實效保健操
定價180元

22 越吃越性福
定價200元

23 荷爾蒙與健康
定價180元

24 越吃越長壽
定價

25 自我保健鍛鍊
定價180元

26 斷食促進健康
定價180元

大展好書　好書大展
品嘗好書　冠群可期

大展好書　好書大展
品嘗好書　冠群可期